Contents

Oasis in the sea

The coral reef is a splendid example of a balanced natural
habitat. Sea fans, anemones and sponges fasten onto the coral.
Crustacea dwell in the many nooks and recesses formed by the
coral heads. Small creatures find nourishment and haven among the
reef growths and in turn provide food for larger animals.
Each species of coral polyp has its own typical growth and
reproduction pattern, forming the various colonies we see in the
seascape above. Some corals branch out into tree-like shapes
while others form convoluted boulders.

The coral reef is an ancient association of life forms
that have been in existence 500 million years. Individual
coral polyps are tube-shaped and range in size from pinhead to
one foot across. The close-up of a colony (left) is four times
life-size. It shows the slit-like mouth opening surrounded
by tentacles that extend to sting and trap food. Cells on the
lower sides and bottom of this animal produce the limestone
that builds islands and reefs. The fringing reef (right)
is formed by literally billions of these tiny creatures.

Coral is fed by water currents that bring it plankton, the
tiny organisms suspended in seawater that sustain even great
whales. Temperatures most favorable to vigorous growth range
from about 75° to 85° F. This need for warm water limits
most reefs to the eastern shores of continents in the
subtropic and tropic zones. Reef coral always has, living within
itself, small plant-like cells called zooxanthellae. Since
these organisms require light in order to live, reef corals are
generally found in water depths of less than one hundred feet.

Roaming
the reef

Floating away the afternoon
with the warm sun at our backs
and the reef below, time
ceases to exist. The soft
white sand bottom reflects
the light so that it shimmers
round from every side.
We sway with the movements
of the sea that give rhythm
to the seafans and gorgonians
beneath us.

Parrotfish nibble daintily
on outstretched branches of
coral while angelfish draw
near the strange visitors.
Our eyes search out the
crevasses and gullies
all curtained and draped
with sponges and algae, red
and purple, green and blue.

Stone flowers: hard corals

Hard corals are the masons of the stone castles that make up the reef. Some colonies of polyps create fragile lacy clusters, while others build massive structures that reach the sea surface from depths of 35 feet.

Brain corals

Structural patterns of this coral resemble the meandering pathways of the human brain. Unlike the brain, the only living parts are on the surface. The polyp grows outward, enlarging the colony by budding and dividing until huge boulders are formed. Coral polyps are extremely long-lived, with a life span of centuries. The smaller brain coral *(Diploria labyrinthiformes)*, contrasts with the bolder convolutions of *Colpophyllia natans*, left and two times life-size below.

Elkhorn coral

The elkhorn coral *(Acropora palmata)* above is a living diagram of
the direction and strength of the currents that run through it.
This master builder of the reef extends dense, palmate branches
that reach a height of 6 to 10 feet. It can cover acres of ground
and form true barrier reefs that stretch unbroken for miles.

Pillar coral

Another name for *Dendrogyra cylindrus* is cathedral coral. These gothic spires are often inhabited by tiny fish with colors of stained glass. This rarely seen coral usually grows apart from the reef. The pillars are very sturdy, but the colony is slow-growing and does not cover a large area, which may account for its scarcity.

Staghorn coral

Though delicate and easily broken at the tips, staghorn coral *(Acropora cervicornis)* is an important reef builder. Like its relative the elkhorn coral, staghorn forms extensive underwater growths, but does not attain as great a height.

Star coral

Living mountains of green velvet host a multitude of creatures. Groupers, moray eels and lobsters find shelter beneath their ledges. Small fish dart about seeking food and defending their territory. Stinging corals may grow upon star coral, along with sea fans and other gorgonians. Star coral *(Montastrea annularis)* establishes one of the most extensive colonies on the reef. The close-up below, four times life-size, shows the polyps retracted into their stony cups. The green coloration is due to algae-like zooxanthellae living within the coral.

Stinging corals

All corals can inflict slow-healing wounds on the diver who brushes against them, but none so painful as that caused on contact with stinging coral. *Millepora alcicornis* (left) and *Millepora complanata* (right) are distant relatives of the stony corals (Anthozoa), but are in the class Hydrozoa. The polyps are very small and do not form visible cups, giving these corals a smoother looking surface than other corals.

Star coral

There are at least eight corals bearing the common name star coral, pointing up the need for scientific names to distinguish between them. The large star coral *(Montastrea cavernosa)* left, is of the same genus as the star coral on page 18, but individual polyps are larger. Star coral (right) of another species, *Dichocoenia stokesii.*

Finger coral

Clubbed finger coral *(Porites porites)* forms small colonies.

Flower coral

Flower coral *(Eusmilia fastigiata)* builds mounds up to 10" across.

Feathers and fans: soft corals

The Gorgons of mythology had snakes for hair and visages so horrid that all who gazed upon them were turned to stone. Their namesakes, the gorgonians, include sea fans and whips. The skeletal structure is resilient and undulates, snakelike, with the movement of water around it.

Gorgonians

Flamboyant in shades of purple, orange, blue,
green and yellow, these plumes, whips and fans
are a conspicuous feature of the coral reef.
Soft corals belong to the same class
as hard corals, Anthozoa, but differ from them in many
ways. The flexible skeletal core is made up of
a tough, horny substance called gorgonin. Each
polyp has eight tentacles, as opposed to six or
multiples of six for hard corals. Food taken
in by any polyp is utilized by the whole
colony in its common digestive system, while
hard corals have individual stomachs. Gorgonians
occur at all depths. The brilliant orange-red
Iciligorgia schrammi (right) was photographed
at a depth of 90 feet, where it looked brown
until the flash revealed its glowing color.

These golden whips and rods are all plexaurid gorgonians.
The polyp structure of eight feathery tentacles is shown
in close-up (above) four times life-size.

Peacock-hued sea fans present themselves broadside to the
prevailing current in order that each polyp may be exposed
to a maximum number of food organisms. *Gorgonia ventalina*
(left) has fastened its short main trunk firmly to a clump
of *Porites astreoides*. The brilliant yellow and green *Gorgonia
flabellum* (below) is usually found in shallow, surging water.

Anemones

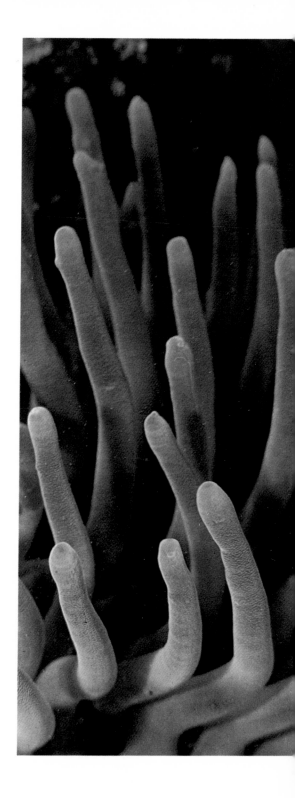

This elegant, translucent creature is much like a coral polyp but lacks its stony skeleton. Most anemones have a tubular body with the mouth centered on a disc atop the free end. Hollow, tapering tentacles armed with stinging cells circle the disc. Anemones secrete a slimy, sticky substance which enables them to secure a footing. When a new site is desirable, the animal "peels" itself off and moves. When moving, some part may be left behind. With some species, a whole new anemone can be regenerated from this part. *Condylactis gigantia* (left and right) is a common shallow-water anemone ranging in color from soft green to lavender.

Sea filters:
the sponges

Though complex in appearance, sponges are simple, multi-celled animals equipped to filter vast quantities of water. Several hundred gallons per day may pass through a sponge in order for it to obtain food and oxygen. Sponges are found in all seas at all depths. They are difficult to identify because they vary in shape, size and color according to the substrate they fasten to and other local conditions. Barrel sponge *(Xestospongia muta)* left, is approximately five feet tall. Tube sponge *(Callyspongia plicifera)* below, is 16 inches high.

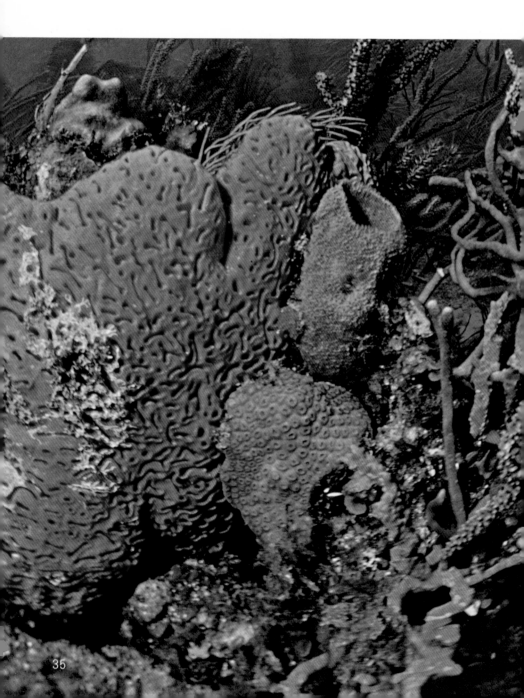

Brilliant colors advertise these sponges, but unpleasant secretions and noxious odors afford some protection for many species. Bright yellow *Verongia fulva* (right) is twice life-size. The orange sponge, genus *Agelis*, is next to *Dasychalina cyathina*, a purple vase sponge.

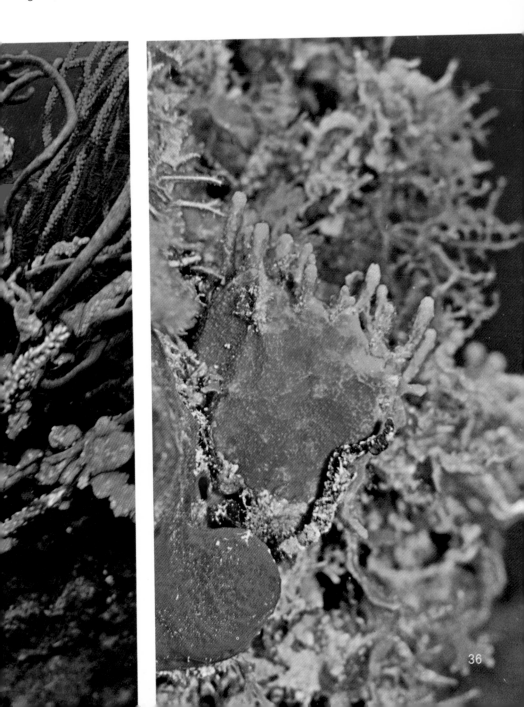

Algae

The base of the marine food chain, algae is the pasturage grazed by herbivores such as snails and parrotfish. Algae are the simplest of all plant forms, lacking roots, stems and leaves. Plants shown here, though given the common names red and brown algae, have colors altered by chlorophyll and other variables. The enlarged photograph (right, about eight times life-size) shows the cells. These marine plants can grow on dead coral surfaces or on seagrass. Many have seasonal cycles like land plants. In a matter of weeks, a whole growth may come and disappear. Other forms of algae range from microscopic diatoms to huge seaweeds.

Plume worms

Concentric twin spirals of feathery gills mark the dwelling place of the serpulid plume worm. This distant relative of the common earthworm remains out of sight in its calcareous tube, permanently imbedded in coral. Only the vivid gill plumes extend outside the tube, to breathe and trap plankton. These plumes retract instantly at the threat of disturbance.

Seven times life-size (left) and twice life-size (above)

Crustaceans

Crustaceans, like their terrestrial counterparts, the insects, have a hard exoskeleton. This protective covering derives rigidity from its lime content. The spiny lobster *(Panulirus argus)* top left, molts its old shell periodically in order to expand within the new covering, and reaches a length of over 20". The tail, that succulent reservoir of sweet meat, is composed largely of muscles used for backward propulsion. The banded coral shrimp *(Stenopus hispidus)* lower left, often performs grooming duties by eating parasites from the mouths of moray eels. This feeding ritual, coupled with its

barber pole stripes, probably accounts for its other common name, barber shrimp. The coral crab *(Carpilius corallinus)* this page, has powerful claws capable of crushing sea urchins and clams.

The long look

Beyond the sun-dappled shallows lies the world of the deep reef. In this blue zone, from 25 to 60 feet deep, only the diver freed from the surface by a self-contained air supply can glide effortlessly for a long look at the intricate wonders of the reef.

Physically fit people of any age with swimming ability can enjoy diving in safety if they take a good course in basic scuba technique, such as those offered by the YMCA or NAUI. This training should include at least one open ocean checkout in 30 feet of water. Most diving accidents are due to human rather than equipment failure. Always dive with at least one other competent diver. Before leaving the boat, check the current. Stay upcurrent of the boat at all times and be certain there is a stern line with floater buoy, should you be swept past the boat on your

return. Make certain the anchor is well secured. A good reef anchor should have a six foot chain between it and the line. Propellors of passing boats are a serious diving hazard. Have a divers flag up to warn that divers are in the water. Wear a safety vest at all times, even when snorkeling. The wise diver wears gloves and does not touch anything unfamiliar. Spearfishing is anti-environmental and not sportsmanlike with scuba. It also attracts predators. Under no circumstances should you kill non-food fish, or allow others to do so.

Reef tenants: the fishes

The fish that inhabit the reef are its greatest adornment. They glisten in the soft blue light as they parade by in bizarre, kaleidoscope dots and stripes, often as eccentric in behavior as appearance.

Parrotfish

An efficient recycling machine, the parrotfish turns coral and rock into fine sand in the process of grazing algae. Females and males often share a color pattern, but an occasional male attains larger size and more brilliant color and is called a terminal-phase male. The stoplight parrotfish *(Sparisoma viride)* below right, may be male or female, while its companion to the left is a terminal male of the same species, reaching about 20 inches. The terminal male redband parrotfish *(Sparisoma aurofrenatum)* left, is a smaller species, about ten inches in length.

Balloonfish

This scaleless fish *(Diodon holacanthus)*
protects itself by ballooning up with
water. This ability, plus a tough, spiny
skin, may deter many predators from
swallowing it.

Trumpetfish

Often encountered standing on its head to
mimic some part of the submarine landscape,
the trumpetfish *(Aulostomus maculatus)*
appears lethargic. Its telescopic snout can
move so rapidly, however, that small fish
and shrimp seem to vanish into its mouth.

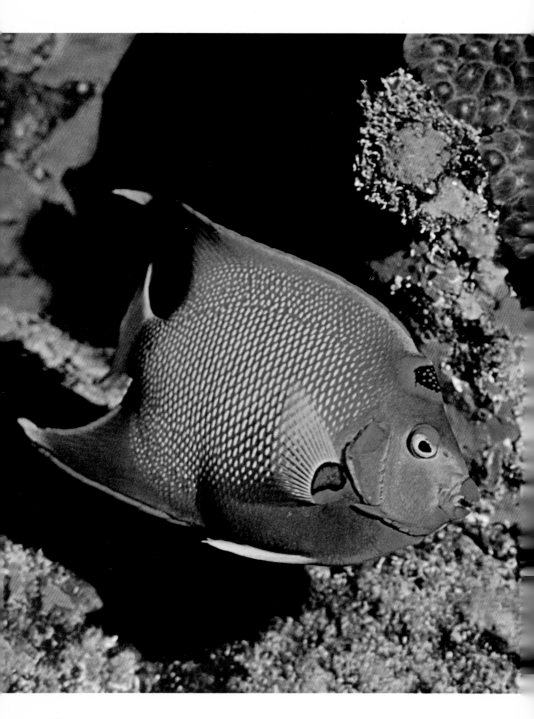

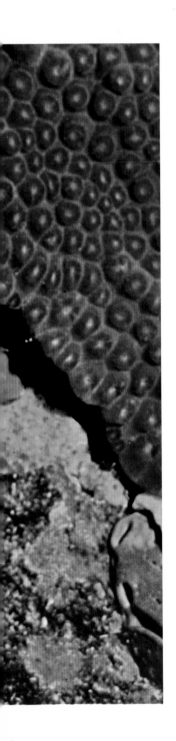

Angelfish

Garbed in a galaxy of colors, the
queen angelfish *(Holacanthus ciliaris)*
derives its imperial status from the
crown on its nape. The electric blue
that spots and rings the crown seems
to pulsate in brilliance. This
lavish coloring blends in surprisingly
well as it flutters among sea fans
or nibbles on bright-hued sponges that
are the mainstay of its diet.
Angelfish are the most curious and
least fearful fish on the reef. They
will hover within a few feet of a
diver, presenting an excellent
target for pictures. The immature
angels, marked with different color
patterns than the adults, are equally
photogenic. Angelfish may reach
a length of 18 inches.

Blue angelfish
Very similar to the queen
angel, the blue angelfish
(Holacanthus isabelita)
top, lacks its crown.

The French angelfish
(Pomacanthus paru) left,
is basically black with
yellow scalloping each
scale. The gray angelfish
(Pomacanthus arcuatus,)
right, sports various
shades of velvety grays.
The boldly striped young
of these two species are
very similar, and only
in maturity are they
easily distinguished from
one another.

Rock beauty

An angelfish of the same genus as the queen angelfish, the rock beauty (*Holacanthus tricolor*) is smaller, reaching one foot in length. The discus-shaped body is orange-yellow with a dark spot that increases in size as the fish grows.

Queen triggerfish

This chameleon of the sea can rotate each eye
independently and effect considerable changes in
color. The two queen triggerfish shown here
(Balistes vetula) have different color patterns.
Vivid blue stripes below the eye remain constant.

Look, but don't touch!

Among the dangers to man in the sea, the most commonly hazardous are of a passive nature. Stinging corals and red fire sponge do not seek out man. If left undisturbed, the spotted scorpionfish *(Scorpaena plumieri)* sits quietly on the sea floor, preying upon small fish and crustacea that venture too near its well-camouflaged exterior. Divers should take care not to touch or step on scorpionfish, as puncture wounds from its spines can cause infection and great pain. Other creatures to be avoided are stingrays that often burrow in the sand, sea urchins and bristleworms.

Sea urchin

The long spined sea urchin
(Diadema antillarum) has
jet black spines that can
penetrate human skin easily
and break off, causing
intense stinging pain.

Bristleworm

The decorative white bristles
of *Hermodice carunculata*
are its armament. These
brittle lengths of glasslike
matter detach with ease upon
contact, and produce severe
pain lasting several hours.

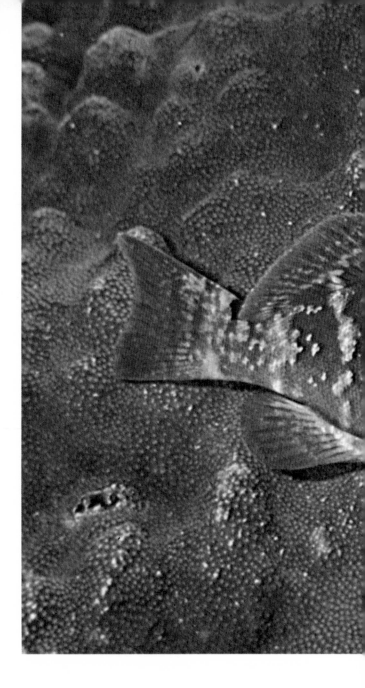

Groupers

The Nassau grouper *(Epinephelus striatus)* exhibits interesting characteristics common to many sea basses. All groupers mature first as females and produce eggs. They change sex later in life to become functioning males. Groupers can affect rapid color changes, going from light to dark in seconds. Nassau groupers may reach a size exceeding three feet in length.

Coney

Both the coney *(Epinephelus fulvus)* and the graysby are less than a foot in length. They have a number of color phases, but the coney usually retains its blue spots.

Graysby

The graysby *(Epinephelus cruentatus)* may vary its ground color from white to brown, its spots from red to dark brown, or even show a banded pattern.

Jewfish

Capable of providing enough food for a good-sized banquet,
this giant sea bass can be recognized by size alone.
The jewfish *(Epinephelus itajara)* may grow to
eight feet and weigh over 700 pounds.

Squid and octopus

Enormous eyes remarkably like man's gleam through the water as waves
of fluorescent colors pulse over the mantle of the popeyed squid
(Sepioteuthis sepioidea), top. Giant squid can reach two tons in weight
and 60 feet in length, but this small reef species is about 15 inches
long. Squid and octopus have a highly developed nervous system and
intelligence superior to other marine life, excepting mammals. When
frightened, they turn white, jet backwards by blasting water through a
siphon in their mantle cavity, and squirt inky fluid to mask odor and
distract the predator. *Octopus vulgaris* (right) often escapes danger
by squeezing its boneless body through extremely small openings.
Both the eight-footed octopus and its fellow cephalopod, the ten-footed
squid, can regenerate lost sucker-studded tentacles.

Safety in numbers:
the schooling fish

Silvery schools of smallmouth grunts
(Haemulon chrysargyreum) are seldom found
more than a few yards from the reef by day.

Goatfish

Rarely exceeding a length of 15",
yellow goatfish *(Mulloidichthys
martinicus)* are nevertheless a
prized fishermen's catch for the
pot. Goatfish probe the sandy sea
floor with their long barbels
searching out small invertebrates
to feed on.

Grunts

Named for the sounds they are
able to produce, grunts hover over
the reef in huge schools during
the day. At night, they spread out
on the sand and grass flats to feed.
The white grunt *(Haemulon plumieri)*
can grow up to 16 inches long.

Spadefish

Curious spadefish *(Chaetodipterus faber)*
swim a silvery circle about a diver.
This species average 15 inches long.

74

Silversides

Immense schools of three to five inch
silversides make up in numbers what they
lack in size. The reef silverside *(Allanetta
harringtonensis)* and the hardhead silverside
(Atherinomorus stipes) form a shimmering
blizzard of motion around a lone diver.

Jacks

These swift-swimming rovers commonly enter the
reef community to feed on resident fish. Bar jack
(Caranx ruber) are strikingly marked with a dark
band extending along the back and crossing down
to the lower lobe of the fin.

Porkfish

Dense, moving schools of fish make it hard for a predator
to single out one fish for attack. More than one genus may
school together. Porkfish *(Anisotremus virginicus)*, one-foot
long members of the grunt family, are usually found in
shallow inshore waters. *Chromis multilineatus*, in left
background, seems to find this an ideal living area as well.

Though guilty of some attacks on humans in poor visibility situations or when speared, the great barracuda (*Sphyraena barracuda*) poses a more serious threat to the digestive tract when eaten than in the open sea. More ciguatera (fish poisoning) has been caused by barracuda than any other fish. These predators may reach a length exceeding six feet, but are seldom encountered more than four feet long.

Rogues' gallery

Shark

Sharks do not dwell on the reef, but, like the bull shark *(Carcharhinus leucas)* only visit occasionally. If divers do not kill fish, the danger posed by sharks may be minimized, as sharks are attracted to an area by the low frequency vibrations and scent trails from wounded fish.

Moray eels

As beautiful and repulsive as the snakes they resemble, these fish are largely nocturnal and secretive by nature. They are harmless to man unless provoked, hiding in crevices and under coral ledges. The goldentail moray *(Muraena miliaris)* left, grows to no more than two feet. The green moray *(Gymnothorax funebris)* below, has awesome teeth and is among the largest of eels, reaching a length of six feet and weight of 25 pounds.

Living jewels:
marine tropicals

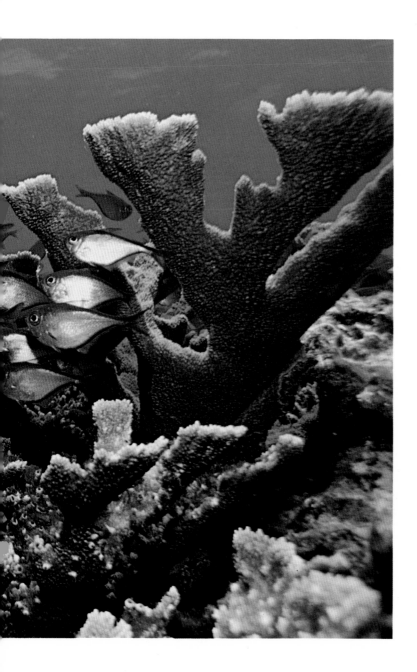

Animated gems that flit about in their coral setting,
marine tropicals are the gaudy embellishment of the reef.
Copper sweepers *(Pempheris schomburgki)* add a metallic luster
to the caves and hollows they usually inhabit.

Hawkfish

Balancing upon its pectoral fins
over a coral rubble-strewn bottom,
the redspotted hawkfish *(Amblycirrhitus pinos)*
is shown approximately twice life-size.

Cardinalfish

The tiny iridescent belted cardinalfish
(Apogon townsendi) grows to only about
2.5 inches. Males of this genus have been
observed incubating eggs orally.

Bluehead wrasse

Bluehead wrasse *(Thalassoma bifasciatum)* afford a confusing example of sex-related color changes. Yellow-phase blueheads (right) may be juvenile or mature females and males. They grow to about five inches, but may be sexually mature as small as one and one-half inches, mating in groups. A small number of males and possibly some sex-reversed females become terminal-phase supermales, developing the colors shown below. The supermale may grow to six inches and always mates singly with a female.

Harlequin bass

Among the smallest of seabasses, the harlequin bass
(Serranus tigrinus) rarely exceeds a length of four inches.
All species of *Serranus* are functional hermaphrodites, with
both eggs and sperm, though they usually pair to spawn.

Cubbyu

The cubbyu *(Equetus acuminatus)* is included in the drum or croaker family, named for the sounds they produce.

Jackknife

Flag-like dorsal fins *(Equetus lanceolatus)* are like that of its cousin, the spotted drum.

Spotted drum

Rarest of this genus, the spotted drum *(Equetus punctatus)* is in the same size range as those above, less than ten inches.

Creole wrasse

Emblazoned with vivid shades of purple, the creole wrasse *(Clepticus parrai)* features an interior of pale blue teeth and bones. This fish attains a length of 10-12 inches.

Glasseye

Retiring beneath its daytime shelter, the glasseye snapper *(Priacanthus cruentatus)* is nocturnal. Shown life-size (left), this member of the bigeye family can grow to 12 inches.

94

Tang

The foot-long blue tang *(Acanthurus coeruleus)* carries a concealed
weapon. Within the white sheath at the base of its tail is a hinged,
lance-like spine. This characteristic gives rise to the family
name, surgeonfish. An intruding fish may be threatened by a display
of the sweeping tail, or actually slashed by this sharp spine.
The young tangs are a striking lemon yellow, developing to blue
as they mature. They browse exclusively on ever-abundant algae.

Neon goby

Mercury-bright markings may be a form of advertising for neon
gobies *(Gobiosoma oceanops)*. Larger fish approach them eagerly
for parasite-picking service, mouth open and gill covers
lifted to facilitate the job. Neon gobies enjoy relative
safety from predation in return, and a meal of parasites.
The cleaning station established on brain coral by these less
than two inch long fish sometimes boasts a waiting line.
The bluehead wrasse *(Thalassoma bifasciatum),* another
parasite-picker, is cleaning the tang shown above.

Butterflyfish

These close relatives of angelfish flit
about the reef, poking elongated snouts
into nooks and ledges in search of the small
invertebrates and plants that make up
their diet. Though they attract attention,
various markings confuse predators.
The characteristic black stripe running
down the face is eye-concealing, making it
difficult to plot which way they are headed.
The foureye butterflyfish *(Chaetodon
capistratus)* top, has a set of false "eyes"
at its rear. The banded butterflyfish
(Chaetodon striatus) below, adds other bold
stripes to further the confusion. Mature
fish reach lengths of four to six
inches and usually travel in pairs.

Squirrelfish

Poised over sponge-encrusted mound coral, the squirrelfish *(Holocentrus rufus)* right, is an impressive sight with its spines extended. Though most of the squirrelfish group are nocturnal, this species is active in the daytime, and is more commonly seen by reef divers. The dusky squirrelfish *(Holocentrus vexillarius)* top, emerges to feed at night. Light of day sends it into hiding in caves and crevices with other nocturnal fish, such as sweepers and bigeyes. *H. vexillarius* reaches a size of about six inches, half the length of *H. rufus*.

Hamlets

Wearing coats of many colors, the hamlets are among the most flamboyant-hued of the seabass family. Shy and retiring, these five to six inch fish dart quickly away if startled. Most of the various color types were formerly considered subspecies of *Hypoplectrus unicolor*, a name retained by the butter hamlet (left). Now recognized as a distinct species, the blue hamlet *(Hypoplectrus gemma)* often swims with and mimics its look-alike, the blue chromis.

Damselfish

Small but pugnacious damselfish will nip at large fish or even divers when their territory is threatened. The male usually stands guard over the dark red to purple egg clusters lest they be gobbled up by other fish. The sergeant major *(Abudefduf saxatilis)* bottom right, abounds on the reef. The yellowtail damselfish *(Microspathodon chrysurus)* below, flashes its metallic blue spots as it browses algae from dead coral surfaces. Both the sergeant major and the yellowtail damselfish reach a maximum size of seven inches. The cocoa damselfish *(Eupomacentrus variabilis)* top right, rarely exceeds four inches in length.

Jawfish

Hovering protectively above its rock-lined
burrow, the tiny jawfish *(Opistognathus aurifrons)*
revolves slowly as it picks off small organisms
passing by. Approximately twice life-size.

Blue chromis

The significance of the "kissing" display put on by
the blue chromis *(Chromis cyaneus)* is not known. Perhaps
it is a form of dispute or a courting ritual. These
bright blue fish edged with black grow to about five inches.

The Living Reef

The dark green waves with emerald hue,
Imbue the beams of day,
And on the wrinkled sand below,
Rolling their mazy network to and fro,
Light shadows shift and play . . .
And here were coral bowers,
And grots of madrepores,
And banks of sponge, as soft and fair to eye
As e'er was mossy bed . . .
Here too were living flowers
Which, like a bud compacted,
Their purple cups contracted,
And now in open blossom spread . . .
And plants of fibres fine, as silkworm's thread;
Yea, beautiful as Mermaid's golden hair
Upon the waves dispread . . .
Beauty and light and joy are everywhere;
There is no sadness and no sorrow here . . .

selections from
Robert Southey, 1838

Index

Photo data

Photographs in The Living Reef were taken over a 15 year period. In this span of time, I have used a vast array of equipment ranging from macro close-up systems to cameras that cover 140°.

My earliest color work utilized a Leica in my Seahawk housing and a Rolleiflex in the classic Rolleimarine housing. With the Rollei, special adaptation enabled me to use 35 mm. as well as the standard 120 size film. When the Nikon came out, I used it in a variety of plastic housings. I now use this camera in the reliable Nikomar aluminum housing and am completely satisfied with it.

The Nikonos amphibious camera has long been a favorite of mine, especially with extreme wide-angle lenses and for macrophotography with precision extension tubes. I like electronic flash for subjects seven feet away or closer and use the Subsea Mark 150. For greater distance, I find the blue-coated flash bulbs best.

Kodachrome II works well for me in clear water with flash. Ektachrome X is good for available light and High-Speed Ektachrome is a must when the light level is low, the water dirty, or the dive deep. With few exceptions, photographs in The Living Reef have been reproduced from 35 mm. film, mostly Kodachrome II.

Many thanks to Jack Wood for art direction, to Marie Wood for editorial assistance, to Lowell Thomas and Richard Chesher who checked our invertebrate information, and to C. Richard Robins who checked our fish data.

We also wish to thank Robert Work, Patrick Colin, Lee Kotowitz, Dennis Opresko, Walter Goldberg, Carl Gage, Paul Dammann, Dick and Rosie Birch, the Coral Reef Park Co., Simba Greenberg, Flint Greenberg, Mimi Greenberg, Bill Crawford, Tim and Annette Healey, John Searle, Tan Airlines, Francis Heusner, Bob Soto, Paul Adams, Jacabo Goldstein, Dave Bridge, W.E. Garrett and the National Geographic Society. None of the foregoing is responsible for any errors this book may contain.